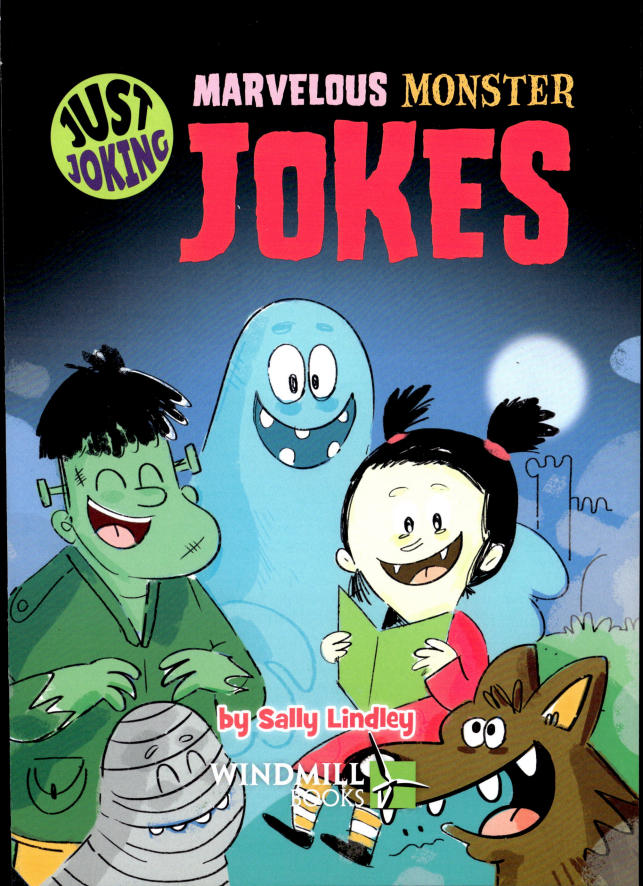

Published in 2017 by Windmill Books, an Imprint of Rosen Publishing
29 East 21st Street, New York, NY 10010

Copyright © 2017 Arcturus Publishing

All rights reserved. No part of this book may be reproduced in any form without
permission in writing from the publisher, except by a reviewer.

Text: Sally Lindley
Illustrations: Fabio Santomauro
Design: Trudi Webb
Editors: Joe Fullman and Joe Harris

CATALOGING-IN-PUBLICATION DATA
Names: Lindley, Sally.
Title: Marvelous monster jokes / Sally Lindley.
Description: New York : Windmill Books, 2017. | Series: Just joking | Includes index.
Identifiers: ISBN 9781508192626 (pbk.) | ISBN 9781508192565 (library bound) | ISBN 9781508192473 (6 pack)
Subjects: LCSH: Monsters--Juvenile humor.
Classification: LCC PN6231.M665 L563 2017 | DDC 808.8'037--dc23

Manufactured in the United States of America
CPSIA Compliance Information: Batch #BS16PK: For Further Information contact Rosen Publishing, New York, New York at 1-800-237-9932

CONTENTS

Madcap Monsters

Why does Dracula wear lace-up shoes?

Because flip-flops look stupid with his tuxedo!

How do you get rid of stinky ghosts?
With scare freshener!

Which monster is horribly untidy?
The Loch Mess Monster!

How do you make a skeleton laugh?
Tickle its funny bone!

What are the best monsters to ask for directions?
Where-wolves!

Grandma ogre: Did you pick your nose?

Little ogre: No, I was born with it!

What do vampires drink at night?

De-coffin-ated coffee!

What did the monster eat after his teeth were pulled?

The dentist!

What's the most important celebration in Egypt?

Mummy's Day!

What kind of music do mummies like?

Wrap music!

Have you heard the monster comedian?

He's awfully funny!

What do you call a 12-foot monster with claws?

"Sir!"

Which dessert makes the swamp monster lick his lips?

Key slime pie!

Why is it difficult to tell twin witches apart?

Because you don't know which witch is which!

WHAT'S BLACK AND WHITE AND DEAD ALL OVER?

A zombie in a tuxedo!

Why didn't the skeleton go bungee jumping?

It didn't have the guts!

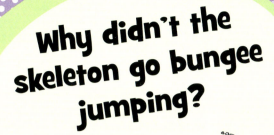

Why can you trust a mummy with your secrets?

They're good at keeping things under wraps!

Where did the zombie's best friend live?

Rotter-dam!

Where did the zombie go to swim?

The Dead Sea!

What's the difference between a dragon and a newspaper?

Have you ever tried to swat a fly with a dragon?

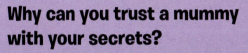

What does an ogre drive?

A monster truck!

Why did the monster throw up after it ate the priest?

Because it's hard to keep a good man down!

What did the ghost write in his girlfriend's Valentine card?

You're simply boo-tiful!

Why did the aliens call their baby "Jupiter"?

Because it was dense and gassy!

WHAT'S THE BEST PLACE TO TALK TO A MONSTER?

From as far away as possible!

Why did all of Dracula's servants quit?

Because of his bat temper!

Why did the ancient Egyptian cross the road?

To get to his mummy!

What do you call an average-size troll?

Medi-ogre!

Why shouldn't you give green vegetables to evil monsters?

Because there's no peas for the wicked!

What do little vampires eat?

Alpha-bat soup!

WHY DID THE MONSTER STOP BITING HIS NAILS?

His mother said they might be rusty!

What did the little ghost say to his best friend?

"Do you believe in people?"

What is a vampire's best-loved sport?

Bat-minton!

What are vampires most afraid of?

Tooth decay!

How do you swap one witch for another?

Just add an "s" to make a switch!

Which extreme sport do monsters like best?

Fright-water rafting!

What do you say to a French skeleton?

Bone-jour!

Why didn't the skeleton go to the party?

It didn't have any body to go with!

What's green, has two heads and six arms, and goes "Beep, beep?"

An alien stuck in a traffic jam!

Who won the Zombie race?

No one, it was a dead heat!

Did you hear about the witch who turned green?

She got broom sick on long journeys!

Why is a yeti like an ox that's swallowed a stick of dynamite?

They're both abominable (a bomb in a bull).

Which monster is really good at science?

Frank Einstein!

How do monster stories begin?

"Once upon a slime ..."

WHY DID THE VAMPIRE NEED MOUTHWASH?

He had bat breath!

Who's the most important player on a monster soccer team?

The ghoul keeper!

Where do you rent a bloodsucking monster?

At a vamp-hire!

Which dance is hard for a vampire to resist?

The fang-dango!

What kind of monster loves to dance to pop music?

A boogie-man!

How can you tell if an alien has used your hairbrush?

It glows in the dark!

ON WHAT DAY DO LITTLE MONSTERS TAKE A BATH?

Scumday!

What's green, has two heads, and goes up and down?

An alien stuck in an elevator!

What type of dog does a vampire have?

A bloodhound!

On what day was the hairy monster born?

Fursday!

Which monster has one eye and one wheel?

A unicyclops!

Which meal do sea monsters like best?

Fish and ships!

Why did the monster buy three socks?

Because he grew three feet!

How does a zombie help you out?

He gives you a hand!

Why did Dracula take cold medicine?

To keep from coffin!

Why didn't the mummy have any friends?

He was too wrapped up in himself.

Gigglesome Ghouls

HOW CaN YOU TELL IF A SKELETON OWNS aN UMBRELLA?

It's bone dry!

How do witches race each other?

They ride vroomsticks!

Where's the safest place to hide from a zombie?

In the living room!

What do monsters eat at the beach?

Lice cream!

What do ghosts wash their hair with?

Sham-boo!

What did the skeleton order at the restaurant?

Spare ribs!

What does Dracula do in the summer?

He goes vamping!

How do monsters cook humans?

They like them terror-fried!

What kind of magic do witches perform using small plates?

Saucer-y!

What kind of books do ghosts read?

Whoooo done its!

Why did the banshee marry a pirate?

So she could wail the seven seas!

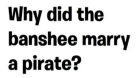

HOW DO YOU MAKE A WITCH JUMP?

Add a "t" to make them twitch.

When is it easy to beat a zombie in an argument?

When it has no leg to stand on!

What did ancient Egyptian monsters call their parents?

"Mummy and Deady"!

How did the monster spike its hair?

With scare gel!

What game do zombies like playing?

Hide-and-shriek!

Did you hear about the ghost who was a big opera fan?

He loved haunting melodies!

What do you call a sprite with a twisted ankle?

A hobblin' goblin!

What do you get if you cross an abominable snowman with a kangaroo?

A big fur coat with pockets!

Why did the cyclops' school lose money?

Because it only had one pupil!

What kind of blood do pessimistic vampires like best?

B negative!

What do you do with a green monster?

Wait until it gets ripe!

Why do novelists like to write in cemeteries?

Because there are so many plots there!

What do monsters eat with their cake?

Eyes-cream!

WHERE DO BABY BANSHEES LEARN TO WAIL? In noisery school!

How do you know the skull won the race?

It was definitely ahead!

How do you get into a haunted house?

With a skeleton key!

What do zombies play in the playground?

Corpses and robbers!

Why was Dracula thrown out of his art class?

He could only draw blood.

Why should you be especially afraid of a vampire dog?

Its bite is worse than its bark!

What did the ogre say when he saw his friend's monster truck?

I'm green with envy!

Why wasn't the zombie chosen to teach at the drama school?

They wanted someone more lively!

What did the vampire say to the invisible man?

Long time, no see!

How do you make a witch scratch herself?

Take away the "w" to make her itch.

WHICH MONSTER NEVER USES DEODORANT?

Stankenstein!

Why did the dragon join a gym?

It wanted to burn some calories!

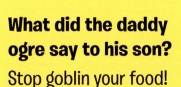

What did the daddy ogre say to his son?

Stop goblin your food!

How does a wizard know what time it is?

He checks his wrist witch!

What advice should you remember if you're running away from a zombie?

Don't go down any dead ends!

Why was the werewolf arrested at the meat counter?

He'd been caught chop-lifting!

WHAT DO YOU CALL A WITCH AT THE SEASIDE?

A sand-witch!

Who saves drowning spirits at the seaside?

The ghostguard!

Why was the swamp monster late for work?

He got bogged down in traffic!

What do you call a haunted hen?

A poultry-geist!

How high do witches fly?
Way up in the atmos-fear!

How do you sign a letter to a monster?

Best vicious!

What's the worst game to play with a huge, angry troll?

Squash!

What type of witch can help you see in the dark?

A lights-witch.

What did the ghost say to the terrified child as it floated across his room?

Don't worry, I'm just passing through!

Did you hear about the overworked zombie?

He was dead on his feet!

What do elves use to make their sandwiches?

Shortbread!

Which ice cream do vampires like best?

Vein-illa!

What do you call a friendly pharaoh?

A chummy mummy!

Why do werewolves get good grades at school?

Because they can always come up with a snappy answer!

WHAT GOES "HA HA, THUNK?"

A monster laughing its head off!

26

How do mummies hide?

They wear masking tape!

When does a zombie go to sleep?

When it's dead tired!

What do you call a witch at the beach who is too scared to swim?

A chicken sand-witch!

What does a headless horseman ride?

A night-mare!

How do vampires wash themselves?

They get in the bat tub!

WHAT DO YOU CALL A WEREWOLF WITH NO MONEY?

Paw!

Did you hear about the monster that listened to classical music all day?

It had a suite tooth!

Did you hear about the witch in the five-star hotel?

She ordered broom service!

What board game do zombies avoid?

Life!

What type of potato does Frankenstein like best?

Monster mashed!

What sport does King Kong like to play?

Ping Kong!

What do you get if you cross a vampire and a criminal?

A fangster!

What do aliens do to congratulate each other?

They give each other a high six!

What does a monster give her husband on Valentine's day?

Ughs and kisses!

Where do clever aliens study?

In a parallel university!

Where did Dracula go sightseeing?

The Vampire State Building!

What does an alien use to keep its jeans up?

An asteroid belt!

Have you heard the new joke about the body snatchers?

I'd better not tell it, you might get carried away!

What do you call a dinosaur that's been on a diet?

The Lot Less Monster!

WHY DO YOU NEVER SEE A FAT VAMPIRE?

Because they eat necks to nothing!

What is a zombie most likely to receive a medal for?

Dead-ication!

What time of day do zombies like best?

Ate o'clock!

Which fruit do vampires like to eat?

Neck-tarines!

Which monster lives in the forest?

Franken-pine!

Who goes to ghost school?

Ghoulboys and ghoulgirls!

Creepy Critters

WHAT DOES A WITCH SAY WHEN SHE'S MADE A CAULDRON FULL OF EYEBALL SOUP?

That should see me through the week!

What does a monster take for a splitting headache?

Superglue!

Does Dracula ever eat steak?

Yes, but very rarely!

What did the werewolf say to the skeleton?

It's been nice gnawing you!

How do you stop a robot from biting its nails?

Replace them with screws!

What do banshees take to the beach?

Sunscream!

What directions did the goblin give to the lost ghost?

Go straight, then make a fright at the next turn!

What do you get if you cross a zombie with a gangster?

Frankenstein's mobster!

Which drink do aliens serve at parties?

Gravi-tea!

What safety device is found in all ghost cars?

Sheet belts!

What did the vampire say to his dentist?

Fangs very much!

What do skeletons say before each meal?

Bone appetit!

Did you hear about the monster that ate a lamp?

It just wanted a light lunch!

Do monsters eat snacks with their fingers?

No, they eat the fingers separately.

WHY WAS THE MONSTER AT THE TOP OF HIS CLASS?

Because two heads are better than one!

Why did the vampire teacher suddenly leave class?

She needed to take a coffin break!

What do spooks put their drinks on?

Ghosters.

How do ghosts make themselves heard in a crowd?

They use a loud-spooker!

Who's in charge of Monster City?

The night-mayor!

Where can you buy cheap zombies?

At a monster sale!

WHICH HOLIDAY DO VAMPIRES LIKE BEST?
Fangs-giving!

Why do skeletons find it easy to stay calm?
Because nothing gets under their skin!

Why should you tell jokes to a ghost?
To lift her spirits!

What day of the week do ghosts look forward to?
Fright-day!

How do you greet a four-headed monster?
Hello, hello, hello, hello!

Where should you send a dirty alien?

Into a meteor shower!

Can a monster jump higher than a tree?

Of course it can. Trees can't jump!

Why were the vampires upside down?

They were just hanging out!

Where do the scariest aliens live?

In a far-off, distant terror-tory!

WHAT DO YOU CALL AN ALIEN WITH NO EYE? "Alen."

Did you hear about the vampire that preyed on polar bears?

It got frostbite!

Why did the witch have sore knees?

She suffered from broom-atism!

What monster likes cleaning?

The Grim Sweeper!

Did you hear about the poltergeist in the china shop?

It had a smashing time!

Why did the witch put her broom in the washing machine?

She wanted a clean sweep!

Why can't skeletons play hymns in church?

Because they don't have any organs!

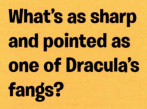

What did the ghost order at the restaurant?

Ghoulash!

What's as sharp and pointed as one of Dracula's fangs?

The other one!

What do you get if King Kong sits on your piano?

Flat notes!

What do you get if you cross an undead creature with a shellfish?

Frankenstein's lobster!

What do aliens use to shave their faces?

Laser blades!

What do monsters eat with their sandwiches?

Ghoulslaw!

What party game do monsters like best?

Swallow the leader!

What happened when the girl vampire met the boy vampire?

It was love at first bite!

WHY SHOULD YOU NEVER LIE TO A MONSTER WITH X-RAY VISION?

Because it can see right through you!

What do you call a monster in a toy car?
Stuck!

Why do Frankenstein's monster's arms squeak?

Because he ran out of elbow grease!

What's a ghoul's best-loved dessert?

Strawberries and scream!

What's it like to have a monster as a pilot?

Terror-flying!

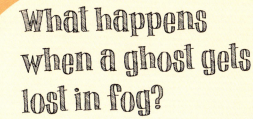

What happens when a ghost gets lost in fog?

He's mist.

WHAT'S BIG AND UGLY AND BLUE?

A monster holding its breath!

What is William Shakespook's most famous play?

Romeo and Ghouliet!

How do monsters travel on business trips?

By scare-plane!

What game do you play with a baby ghost?

Peeka-boo!

What do vampires do at the circus?

Go for the juggler (the jugular)!

Which sweet treats do aliens like best?

Martian-mallows!

What party game do ghouls play?

Musical scares!

Why don't witches need dictionaries?

Because they're very good at spelling!

Why are little monsters green?

Because they're not ripe yet!

What do ghosts like to eat for dessert?

I scream!

Why did the one-armed monster go into town?

To visit the second-hand shop!

Why did the girl want to kiss Dracula?

She was batty about him!

Why should a mummy be careful on its day off?

So it doesn't unwind too much!

Did you hear about the single monster who tried online dating?

She was looking for an edible bachelor!

HOW DO YOU GET A BABY ALIEN TO SLEEP?

Rocket!

What do witches like on their sandwiches?

Scream cheese!

What do you call a vampire that lurks in the kitchen?

Spatula!

What do you shout at a vampire wedding?

Coagulations!

What can you find between King Kong's toes?

Slow runners!

Who did the Zombie invite to his party?

Anyone he could dig up!

WHAT DOES A ZOMBIE READ FIRST IN THE NEWSPAPER?

Its horror-scope!

What goes, "Boohoo, squelch?"

A monster crying its eyes out!

Why didn't Baron von Frankenstein get lonely?

Because he was good at making new friends.

What happens when a witch on a broomstick brakes suddenly?

She flies off the handle!

Who works on a haunted ship?

A skeleton crew!

How do you keep a werewolf from attacking you?

Throw a stick and shout "Fetch"!

Which place do skeletons like to visit?

Death Valley!

How does Frankenstein's monster sleep at night?

Bolt upright!

What kind of cup does a skeleton drink from?

Bone china!

What happens if a green dragon paddles in the Red Sea?

It gets its feet wet!

Further Reading

Dahl, Roald. *Roald Dahl's Marvellous Joke Book.* Puffin, 2012.

Simon, Francesca. *Horrid Henry's Jumbo Joke Book.* Orion Children's Books, 2015.

Weitzman, Ilana. *Jokelopedia.* Workman, 2013.

Glossary

banshee A spirit with a loud, wailing voice.

cyclops A giant one-eyed monster.

ghost The spirit of a dead person who haunts the living.

mummy A body from ancient Egyptian times that's been preserved and wrapped in bandages.

ogre A man-eating giant.

vampire A dead person who has come back to life as a monster. A vampire feeds on the blood of humans, biting their necks with their sharp canine teeth. It can also transform into a bat.

werewolf A person who regularly changes into a wolf, usually when there's a full moon.

witch A woman with magical powers who can cast spells and ride on a broomstick.

zombie A dead person who has been turned into a monster. Zombies feed on human brains.

Index